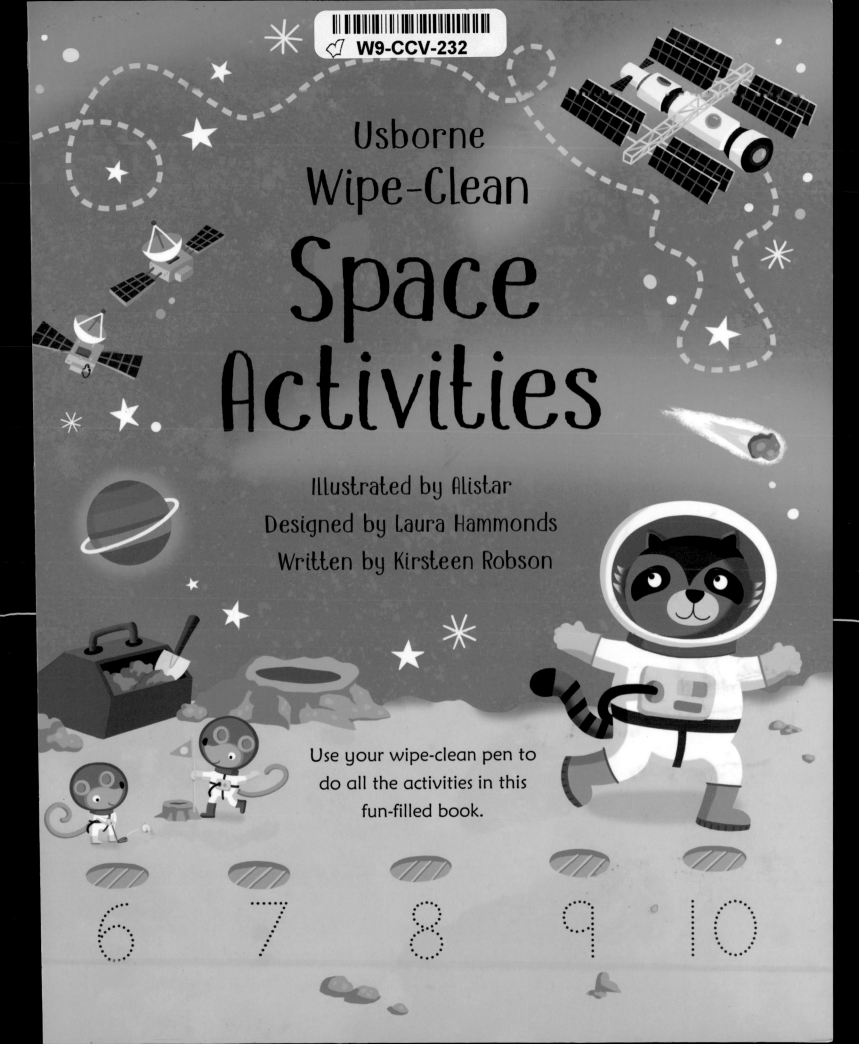

# Usborne
# Wipe-Clean
# Space
# Activities

Illustrated by Alistar

Designed by Laura Hammonds

Written by Kirsteen Robson

Use your wipe-clean pen to do all the activities in this fun-filled book.

# Getting ready

Spot 4 differences between these space suits.

Follow the trails to see what each mouse is planning to take into space.

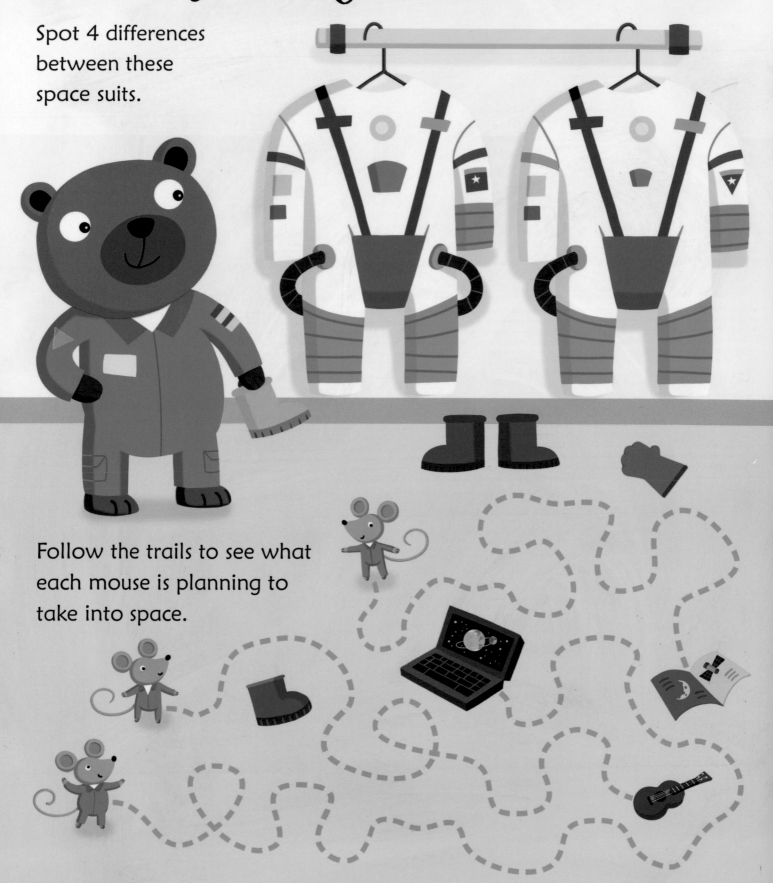

Find and circle 6 boots.

Draw around the picture that does not match the others.

Draw over the dots to finish the helmets.

# Rocket launch

Use the pen to show the astronauts' bus the way to the red rocket.

Spot 5 differences between these rockets.

Draw over the dots to finish the dishes of the radio telescopes.

Trace over the numbers. Then, say them out loud to count down to blast-off.

5 4 3 2 1

# Ground control

Finish the blast-off smoke by drawing over the dots.

Write an X on the little picture that is missing from Berry's screen.

Berry

Draw over the trails to see which satellite went in a full circle around planet Earth.

Find and circle 6 pens.

Draw lines between the half faces that match.

# Up and away

Write an X below the satellite that does not match the others.

Connect the dots to finish the rocket.

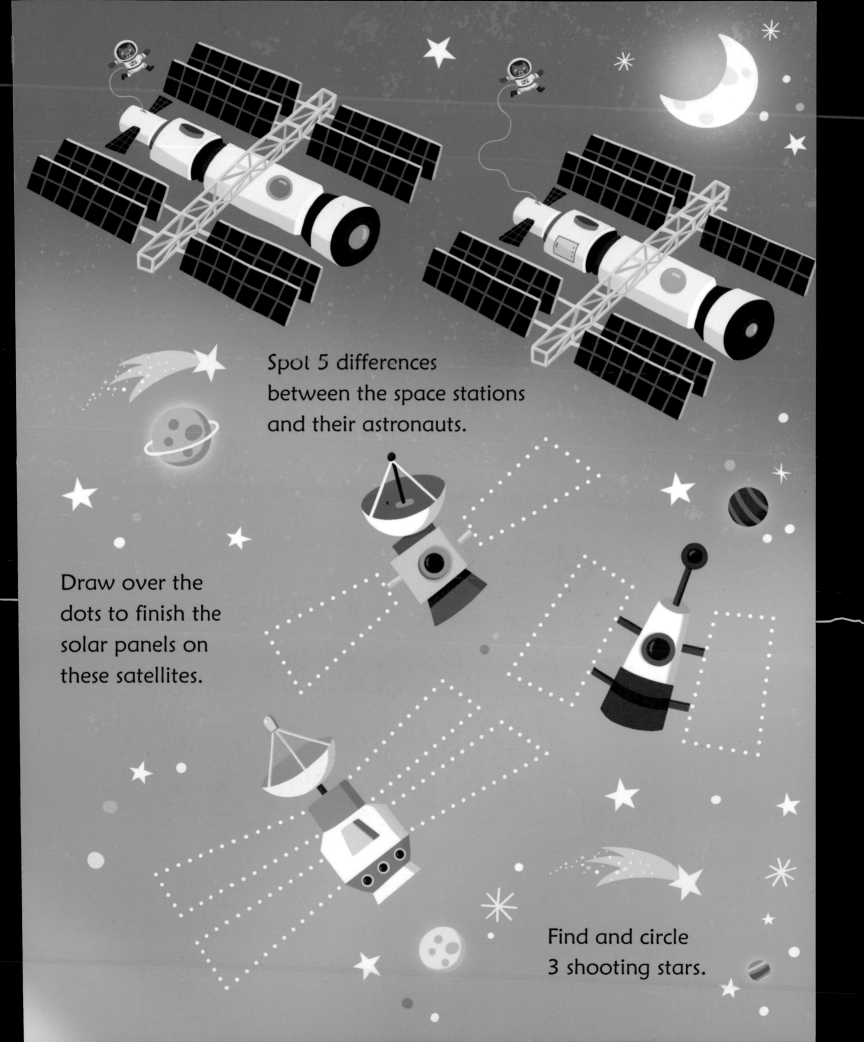

Spot 5 differences between the space stations and their astronauts.

Draw over the dots to finish the solar panels on these satellites.

Find and circle 3 shooting stars.

# In the space station

Draw lines between
the socks that match
each other.

Barney

Trace over the dots to
finish Barney's guitar.

Draw over the dots to finish Buzz's bed.

Buzz

Find and circle 8 toothbrushes.

Follow the trails to see which fruit each mouse will eat.

# Space walk

Draw the missing part of Cosma's yellow tether.

Connect the dots in order to finish the space station.

Cosma

Spot 4 differences between Buzz and Barney.

Buzz

Barney

Draw over the dots to finish the handles and hatches.

Follow the trails to see which tool is tied to Ravi's space suit.

Ravi

# On the Moon

Use the pen to show Buzz the way across the Moon back to the lunar module.

Buzz

Count the rocks in each pile, then trace over the numbers.

3    5    4

Lunar module

Draw over the dots to finish the craters.

Bonny

Draw 3 more of Bonny's footprints in the moon dust.

# Exploring space

Draw over the dots to finish the planets.

Trace the trails to see which planet each spacecraft goes to.

Find and circle 4 comets, like this.

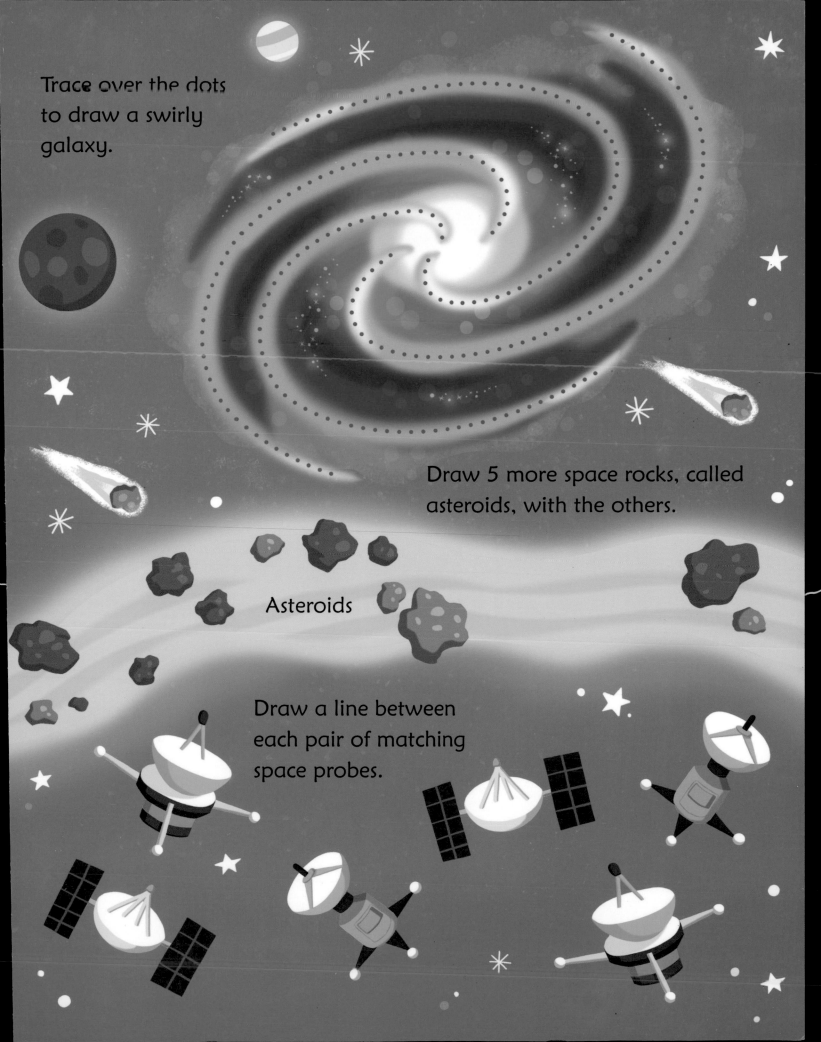

Trace over the dots to draw a swirly galaxy.

Draw 5 more space rocks, called asteroids, with the others.

Asteroids

Draw a line between each pair of matching space probes.

# Life on the orange planet

Use your pen to show Barney the way to Cosma, to see what she's found.

Barney

Draw over the dots to finish the wheels.

Count the plants growing in each container. Then, trace over the numbers.

8    6    7

Connect the dots to finish Bonny's greenhouse.

Find and circle 3 friendly aliens.

Bonny

Cosma

Spot 6 differences between these surface explorers.

# The sky at night

Fill the sky by drawing 5 more stars and 2 more planets.

**Planet**

**Star**

Draw over the dots to finish the Moon.

Circle the sky map that does not match the others.